looking at paintings

about this book

Paintings are like people: they can speak to you, make you feel happy, angry, shocked or calm. They might startle you or impress you, make you laugh or cry. They help you to see places you may never visit, meet famous people in history, make up scenes and stories in your imagination.

This book is all about enjoying paintings. How would you answer if someone asked you, 'What did you think about that picture on the cover?' This book will show you how to look at paintings and how to find words to describe what you see. You'll discover why an artist paints a picture and how he makes all the parts fit together.

There are lots of games and quizzes, too, so you can play detective with pictures. Look for ✱ the sign to see what they are.

Best of all, you'll discover things about yourself and others. No one feels exactly as you do, and the way you react to pictures will be special and different. Looking at pictures is not as easy as watching television but you'll enjoy it more. Try it and see!

Consultant *Terry Measham*
Assistant Keeper
Tate Gallery

Text written by *Frances Kennet*
Terry Measham
Illustrated by *Malcolm Livingstone*

Editor-in-chief *Beverley Hilton*
Editor *Wendy Boase*
Art director *Amelia Edwards*
Researcher *Linda Proud*

Where to look

Of all the pictures you've ever seen, which do you like best? Maybe it's a poster on your wall, or a postcard, or an illustration in a book. If you're lucky enough to live near a gallery or a museum, perhaps it's a famous original painting. Have you ever looked really closely at that favourite picture, or thought about how or when it was made?

How to see

Usually, when people look at a picture, their eyes flit about to get a vague idea of what is going on.

Maybe at first glance you start by loving the colours, or the shapes, or the special feelings a picture stirs up in you. That's a good way to begin. But if you look really closely at pictures and learn something about how they are painted, the pictures will 'speak' to you.

Have a look at *A Winter Scene with Skaters* on pages 4–5. At first, you notice lots of people skating, a big building and a lovely tree. Now have a closer look. Does the picture suggest noises to you? Perhaps the sound of ice cracking, or children laughing, or skates going swish-swish across the ice? See how your imagination begins to work when you give the painting a chance to speak?

Make a view-finder*

Sometimes there is so much to look at in a picture that you want to concentrate on a bit at a time. A little bit of a picture is called a *detail*. Use a view-finder to study details.

1. On a piece of thin cardboard 10cm square, measure and mark 2cm in from the edge. Pencil a line through all the marks.

2. Then draw a coloured line as shown. Cut along the colour to make two L-shaped hooks.

3. Move your hooks about to make the view-finder bigger, smaller, or a different shape. Use them to look closely at real pictures in a gallery or at reproductions in a book.

The *original* painting is the one created by the artist. It is often very valuable because it is the only one in the world.

In the art gallery or museum, where the original usually hangs, someone takes a *photograph* of the painting.

The photographic film is used to make hundreds and hundreds of *prints* or *reproductions* of the original painting.

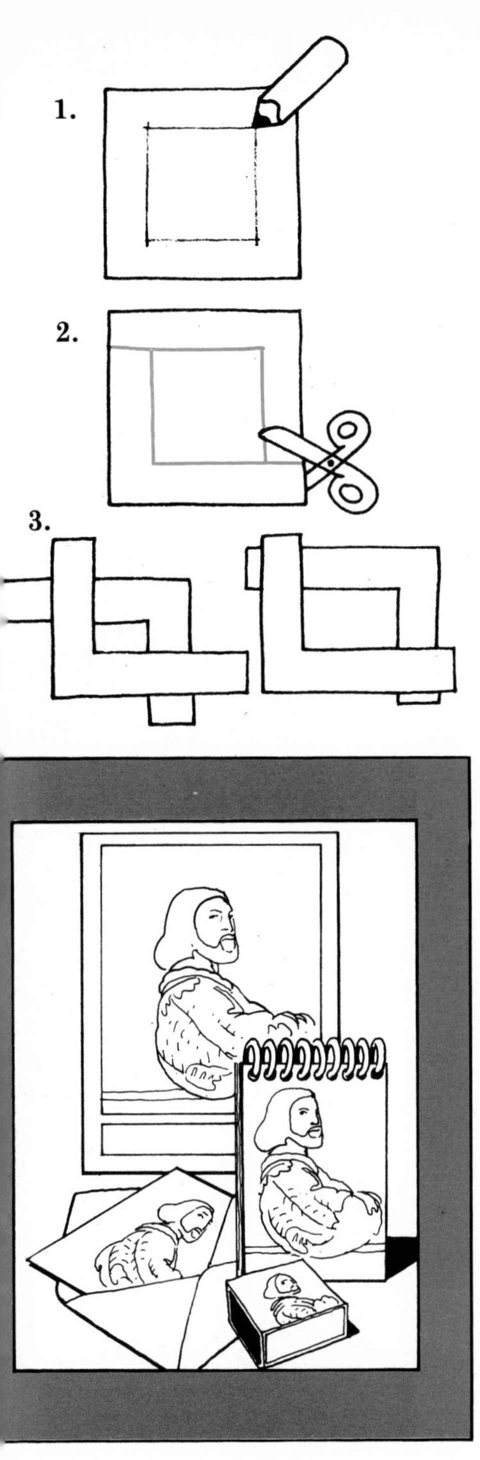

The original painting can be reproduced in books or as posters and postcards which you can put on the wall.

How big is the original?

The prints you see in books or on postcards are often much smaller than the original painting. When you go to a gallery or a museum, there'll be lots of surprises!

Some of the original paintings printed in this book might take up a whole wall of your bedroom or even the classroom wall at school. For instance, the picture on pages 12–13 of the people swimming and sunbathing looks small enough to cover up with your hands. But the real painting is huge—2 by 3 metres. In this book, in fact, only the round skating picture on pages 4-5 and the Persian picture on page 7 are about the same size as the original paintings.

Captions to help

The caption for each picture in the book tells you how big the original painting is. It also gives you the picture's title, the date it was painted, and the name of the painter.

If you look carefully at the pictures themselves, you might find the painter's signature. In the front of the skating picture on pages 4-5, you will see the letters H.A. standing for Hendrick Avercamp. They've been worked into a neat little design called a *monogram.*

Skating in the frosty air

There is so much happening in this little picture of a winter scene: people skating, people falling over, people pushing carts, sitting about or just looking! The Dutch artist who painted it made the picture look crowded and busy. In fact the painter, called Hendrick Avercamp, couldn't talk. This might explain why he liked to share all the things he noticed. He could then say, 'Look at that' in pictures instead of words.

What's everybody doing?

Can you see a boy throwing snowballs at a girl or a horse-drawn sleigh moving across the ice? Do you see a man tying a woman's skate for her? If you look very closely you'll see someone at a window and three other people sitting on a boat.

Far, far away

The painting is only 41cm in diameter—a little larger than you see it here—and yet everything is so clear that you can spot things even in the distance. It's like gazing through a telescope. Look, there's a church a long way off, and people seem to be walking for miles across the ice.
To get this deep, distant look, Hendrick Avercamp painted big people and trees in the front of the picture and made everything else look smaller. Measure the tree halfway back at the right-hand side and compare it with the tree at the front. You'll see that it is only one-third the size. The proper word for showing distance in a painting is *perspective.*

Look again!

Did you notice the man crouched by the tree, right at the front of the picture? The front of a painting is called the *foreground.* And can you see a group of grand people dancing? They are in the *middleground* of the picture. Then there's a castle, and further off, the church, more people and another sleigh. These smaller things are in the *background* of the picture.

Bring the people to life*

Can you make up an imaginary story about some of the skaters in the middleground? Which people do you think live in the castle and which live in town?

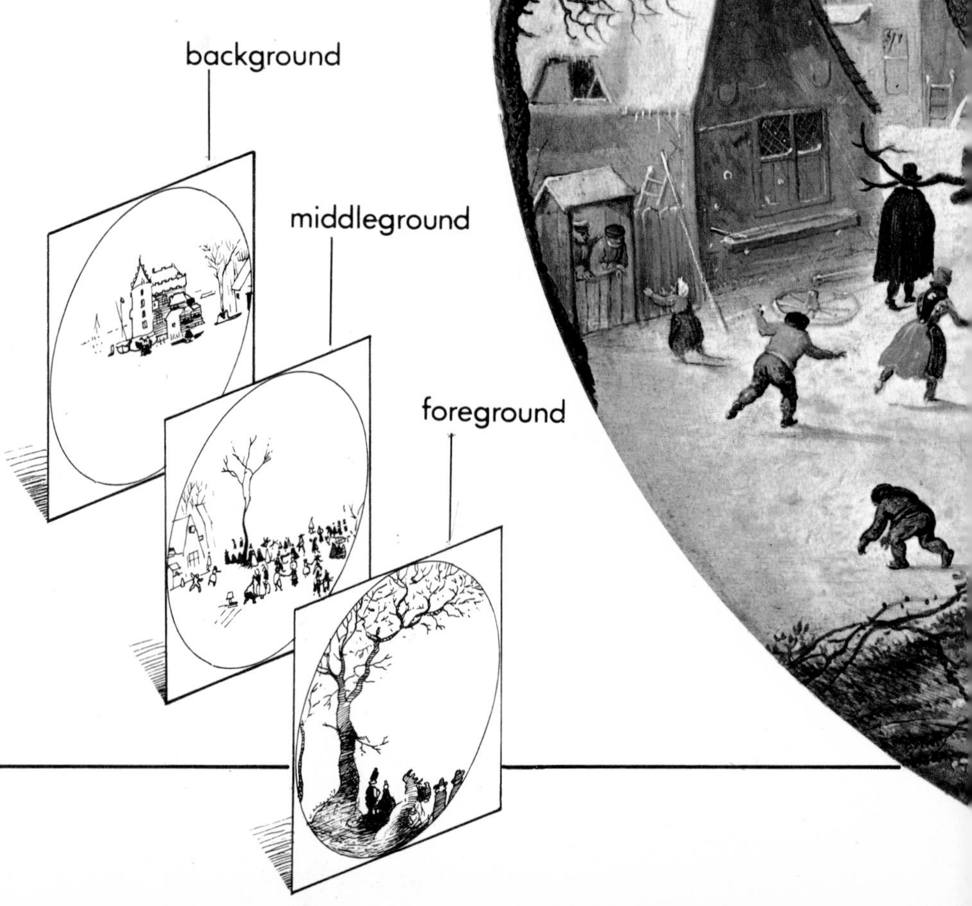

A Winter Scene with Skaters
by Hendrick Avercamp
painted about 1609
size: 41cm diameter

The story of a deadly rose

Here is a mysterious picture. A king sits on a throne with his courtiers around him. On the floor a man lies dead. See how his turban has fallen off? There is a rose near his body. Another man looks on with a wicked grin—he might even be clapping his hands in glee. All the other people look amazed.

Yet you cannot tell the whole truth just by looking at the picture, however hard you try. That's because this picture is an *illustration* for a book. It was painted over four hundred years ago in Persia. (Persia is now called Iran.) The picture makes much more sense when you know the story that goes with it—and here it is.

Once upon a time...

Hundreds of years ago, when Persian Sultans ruled huge empires, two doctors had a competition to become the king's favourite. The first doctor—or physician as they are sometimes called—made a deadly pill from a long list of secret ingredients. It caused fearful stomach aches and fits which killed people. This doctor dared his rival to take the pill. The second physician swallowed it with a smile. He had already taken a magic pill of his own and the deadly medicine had no effect at all.

The Sultan and his court watched eagerly as the second physician plucked a beautiful red rose from the garden. He kissed the petals, whispered a spell into the heart of the flower, and offered it to his enemy. When the first doctor raised it to his lips, he immediately fell down dead. His cunning rival had won.

What the Sultan saw

This is the scene the Persian artist, Aqa Mirak, chose to illustrate in the story book. He wanted to please his Sultan, Shah Tahmasp of Tabriz, so he painted the Sultan of the story to look like the Shah himself. You can see him sitting on his throne under a canopy.

In Persia, people used to sit on cushions instead of chairs. They put their books on to a stand made of carved wood.

The artist wanted Shah Tahmasp to enjoy looking at the ducks in pond, the beautiful tiles on the floor, the flowers in the garden and a traveller's horse in the distance. You couldn't see all these details at once if you stood in one place and looked at the scene. But then, Aqa Mirak didn't worry very much about perspective: he was more interested in getting all these things into his picture.

Imagine the Shah turning the pages of the small, leather-bound book decorated with gold. He would probably smile with pleasure at the beauty of *The Physicians' Duel.*

Colours like jewels

Aren't the colours beautiful? It's like looking into a little jewel box. The colours really glow because they were made from precious stones and costly metals. The green of the Sultan's tunic may be made from a stone called malachite, crushed to a powder and mixed with gum to make a paint. Real silver and gold were beaten to a fine film and also added to the painting. All these rich materials made the book a worthy gift for the Shah.

The Physicians' Duel
by Aqa Mirak
probably painted between 1539–1543
size: 29 x 21cm

War and pain

This picture shows you the pain and suffering of war. A woman screams in agony, her dead child in her arms. A horse rears in torment, a spear through its body. A man lies dying, his broken sword in hand. On the right a woman with her clothes on fire falls from a burning house. Everything looks ugly and distorted.

A town called Guernica

The picture was painted by Pablo Picasso in 1937. The painter was extremely angry about the civil war that was tearing apart his country, Spain. He was especially horrified by the news of a savage and senseless bombing attack by airplanes on a little town called Guernica (pronounced *Gernicka*). Picasso painted this picture to show how ugly war is and how it damages and destroys—and he named the picture after the town. *Guernica* is a huge picture— bigger than the wall of an ordinary sitting-room.

Listen to the sounds

There are no colours in this picture: only blacks, whites and greys. Maybe the painter felt that colours are too beautiful for such a serious subject. Can you hear some of the dreadful noises—the screams, shouts, and groans? You can see that most of the people and animals have their mouths open as if they are screaming in pain. The artist also made everything look broken, crooked and ugly. What sounds and feelings do the criss-cross lines and shapes suggest to you?

The painter's mood

Perhaps the two strongest feelings expressed by *Guernica* are 'I am angry' and 'I am hurt'. How has the artist passed on his mood to you?
You have heard the awful sounds, and noticed the sharp outlines and lack of colour. Now look at the faces. They are just big white shapes with staring eyes and yelling mouths. You can see two eyes in every head, no matter which way it is facing. Like a dead person's stare, the eyes are open and fixed in terror.
At the top of the picture dangles a naked electric light bulb. This glaring light reaches out to reveal the horrors of war. The rays of light from the bulb are like sharp, jagged teeth. The painter made them spiky to set our nerves on edge.
All these details helped Picasso tell you that a terrible thing was happening in this town.

Speaking to everyone

Have you ever seen a news film of a war going on? Have you thought how people and animals are hurt in wars? Although Picasso made his picture because of what was happening in Spain, *Guernica* could be a picture protesting about all wars. That is one reason it has become famous—people all over the world can look at it and understand what the artist is saying.

Guernica
by Pablo Picasso
painted 1937
size: 3·5 x 7·8 metres

A double celebration

This painting by Carlo Crivelli looks complicated at first glance. That's because the artist put two special stories together in his picture.

The Annunciation

The first is the story of the Annunciation, which comes from the Bible. 'Annunciation' is just another word for 'news' or 'announcement'. It is about the Angel Gabriel's visit to the Virgin Mary to tell her that she had been chosen by God to give birth to his son, Jesus.
There's the angel kneeling in the street. And there's Mary, inside the house, with her head bowed in prayer.
But the scene doesn't look at all like Palestine, the Middle Eastern country in which Mary lived. Instead of hot, dusty streets there are cool, stone pavements and potted plants. You can guess from the fine clothes and richly decorated buildings that the scene is set in some other time and place. And that brings us to the second story!

In 1482 the little Italian town of Ascoli was given certain rights of self-government by the Pope. The people of Ascoli first heard the news on March 25th—the day when people celebrate the Angel's visit to Mary.
See how cleverly the artist linked the story of the Annunciation with the news about Ascoli's independence? He painted the Angel Gabriel kneeling before Mary's house with Saint Emidius, the patron saint (or special protector) of the town. The Saint holds in his hands a model of Ascoli. He is showing it to Gabriel as if to say 'Look at our town. We are so proud of it!'

A town within a town

The model of Ascoli shows that it was a strongly fortified town. Look at the defence tower and the sturdy gateway set into the protective wall.
Crivelli also put a lot of other details into this tiny part of his picture. There are windows, doorways and arches. You can even see the lines in the brickwork and the patterns on the roofs.

Learning about the past

Carlo Crivelli's painting looks old and historical now, but it tells us something about Italy in his own time—the 15th century. The citizens who have come out to hear the news are wearing their ordinary clothes. The Virgin Mary looks like a noble lady of the town with her pretty dress and luxurious house. This picture tells us what the clothes, the furniture, and the houses were like. Since photography wasn't invented until about 100 years ago, pictures like this reveal a lot about the past.

Detailed designs

Crivelli must have loved making patterns. You almost notice the buildings and the lovely designs before you notice the people in the picture.
Look at the carved patterns on the pillars of Mary's house. There are more running round the first floor balcony. Then there are patterned ceilings, carpets, clothes and a curtain. Even the arched bridge is decorated with elaborate designs.

Count the patterns*

How many different patterns are there? Don't forget to count the peacock's tail!

The Annunciation with Saint Emidius by Carlo Crivelli painted 1486 size: 2·1 x 1·5 metres

OPVS·CARO
LI·CRIVELLI
VENETI
1486

A lazy summer's day

Can you imagine how hot the hottest summer day can be? If you look at this picture, you can almost feel that kind of heat. This painting shows some people lazing away a hot afternoon. A few are resting or bathing, and others are yachting, punting and rowing. The boy in the orange hat could be whistling or calling to a friend. But all this activity is very slow. You can't see any details in the faces or the clothing of the figures on the river bank; but they look lazy and still—they might even be dozing off in the sun.
There are no clear details in the scenery, either. Everything looks hazy. But notice how the sunlight dances on the trees and how it makes the water shimmer in a thousand places.
And can you see the smoke floating up into the sky from those distant chimneys? There's hardly a breath of wind.
The artist painted a picture of stillness and peace.

The bold young artist

The French artist, Georges Seurat, painted the *Bathers at Asnières* when he was twenty-four years old. At that time most big paintings were of gods and goddesses or of great scenes from history. But Seurat did something unusual: he painted a very large picture of ordinary people enjoying themselves. (The figures in the painting are the same size as real people.)

Arranging the people

To get the feeling of a sunny atmosphere, Seurat stood on the river bank at Asnières (a suburb of Paris) to sketch the colours of the scene. Back in his studio, he made black crayon drawings of people.
When he began to paint the picture, Seurat treated it a bit like a huge stage set. He painted the scenery, then he arranged the figures in it.

New ways with colour

Seurat tried to paint colours exactly like the ones that he noticed when he stood on the river bank at Asnières.
Look closely at the picture and you will find that he used criss-cross strokes in various colours for the grass. He painted smooth thick lines of colour for the water. Both the grass and the water seem to reflect warm yellow sunlight.
But Seurat also experimented with combinations of colour. The boy's orange hat is made up of tiny dots of different colours crowded together.
Later on, Seurat painted all his pictures by making forms and shapes out of thousands of little coloured dots.

Experiment with dots*

If you have lots of patience, you could try painting a little dot picture of a hat. Put yellow and blue dots very close together so that they merge into green.

Bathers at Asnières by Georges Seurat painted 1883–4 size: 2 x 3 metres

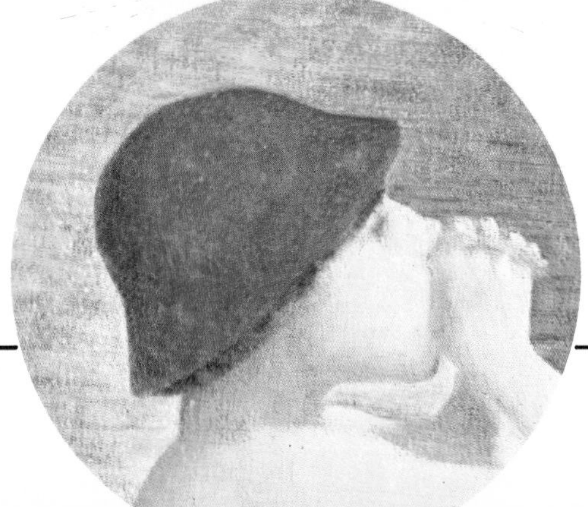

Look carefully at the boy's hat. It's not like the rest of the picture. See how dots of colour merge together into orange? Seurat re-painted the hat this way a long time after he had actually finished the picture.

Sinbad goes to sea

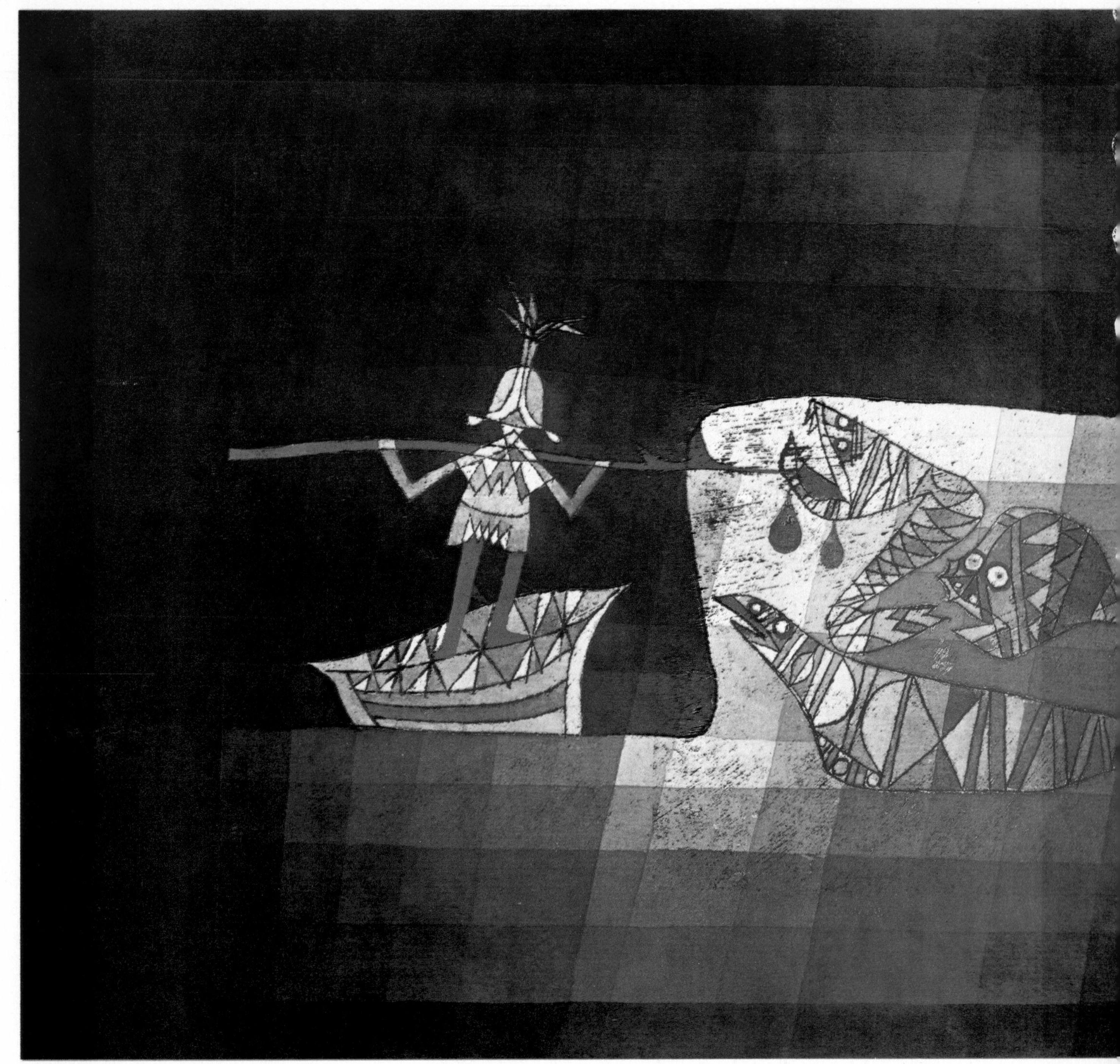

Sinbad the Sailor
by Paul Klee
painted 1923
size: 38 x 52cm

Here is a painting of a little stick-fisherman and three very large fish. Do you think it's amusing that the fish look big enough to swallow both the man and his boat? And isn't the fisherman a rather strange character? Look at those spiky feathers on his head and the zig-zag patterns on his clothes. The boat, too, is much smaller than any ordinary fishing boat. Look how the man, his boat and the fish are all placed in an ocean of coloured squares. No ocean really looks like this.
In fact, nothing in the picture looks realistic.
Can you imagine why Paul Klee (pronounced *Clay*), chose to paint his picture this way?

A magical tale

Sinbad the Sailor is a mythical person and the stories about him are full of magic. In Klee's picture you can tell that Sinbad is harpooning a fish, but neither the man nor the fish looks real. That's because the artist was painting a fable—a kind of fairy-tale—and not a real scene.

Was the painter having fun?

Look at the three fish. Although each one is different, the patterns of their scales match each other. And what about the pattern on Sinbad's shirt—it matches the pattern on his boat. Have you ever heard of a sailor who painted his boat to match his clothes?
Perhaps Klee was simply having fun making colourful designs and shapes.

Panels of colour

Notice how the sea changes colour as your eyes move from one square to another. Klee carefully graded his colours from deep blues and browns at the edges to light blues and white at the centre. In this way he suggests the rise and fall of the ocean, and how its colour changes all the time.
Follow the lines of the squares to see how they join up with the patterns on Sinbad, his boat, and the fish. It looks as if the artist played a game with his coloured checks.

The thoughtful artist

Klee's painting certainly doesn't look solemn, does it? The artist enjoyed making his colourful patterns. But he also thought seriously about man and nature. Klee believed that all living creatures exist together in balanced harmony. That helps to explain why he built everything in his picture into one harmonious pattern.

Trace the lines*

Put a sheet of tracing paper over one of the fish, and then trace all the lines that make up its body. You'll see that Klee's patterns are like tiny fish bones.

Now what would you say?

Here you see the sizes of the pictures compared with the children looking at them. Would you agree with any of these comments about the pictures?

Guernica

'It looks like a puzzle.'

'It's spooky.'

'The horse looks like newspaper writing.'

'He must have been really angry to paint a picture that big.'

'I understand what he's saying, but it still looks silly.'

'That's the picture that will make me go away and think.'

'It looks like it's from a comic book.'

The Annunciation

'The lady must be holy— she's got a plate on her head.'

'I'd feel a stranger in that scene.'

'Everything looks rich.'

'It looks like a picture from another country.'

'Look at the size of that peanut!'

The Physicians' Duel

'I thought a 'duel' meant with swords. Poison is different.'

'It's beautiful. I love the detail and colour.'

'It looks flat. The people are standing on each other's heads.'

'It's like a cartoon because it's telling a story.'

A Winter Scene with Skaters

'I love it because skating is fun and I can imagine it.'

'It's like looking at a scene through a small hole.'

'The tree's haunted and misty.'

'I like the way the view gets smaller as it goes away.'

'The poor man in the front looks cold— he's hunched up.'

Bathers at Asnières

'It looks as though he's put the colour on with a knife.'

'It makes me want to go swimming.'

'It's boring because the people look so posed.'

Sinbad the Sailor

'It's an imaginary land— you don't have zig-zag fish.'

'The painter had a bad dream.'

'It looks like it's in a cinema because the edges are dark.'

Everybody's different!

If you half-close your eyes and look at this picture a wonderful thing happens: it glows with light and movement. See the way the grass seems to shine and change colour as the breeze blows across it?
The artist, Claude Monet (pronounced *Mon-nay*) was fascinated by the way light falls on plants and water. He wanted to tell you how a lilypond looks on a warm day.
Monet didn't show you any precise details. You can't see the leaves of the grass, the petals of the flowers, or the branches of the trees. But you can really feel how lush and strong the grass grows round the water's edge, and how the light dances across the pond.

Light and colour

The Water-Lily Pond is a picture of Monet's own garden which he planned and built himself. The artist stood in the garden and painted the colours of the lily-pond just as he saw them.
You can't find any black in the picture, can you? All the shadows are made up of blues, greens and other dark colours. Monet enjoyed piling rich colours into his painting. See how his brushmarks of colour mingle to give you a vivid impression of light falling on the scene?

The Water-Lily Pond
by Claude Monet
painted about 1899
size: 88 x 92cm

A garden of patterns

Look at the trees and flowers in *The Physicians' Duel.* You can see every detail, but the garden looks 'unreal' compared with Monet's. That's because Aqa Mirak loved making designs on all the surfaces of his picture. He was not interested in showing light and movement.

The delicate wooden bridge

Now look closely at Monet's bridge. The bridge is a sign that people do go into the garden, even though we see nobody in the picture. But it is a flimsy-looking bridge, isn't it? You can't see any supports. And you can't see where the bridge begins and ends. It seems to float above the water just as the lilies are floating on the pond. Monet was not concerned with showing the construction of the bridge—it is the play of light and shadow on it that really caught his interest.

A bridge of solid stone

Remember the bridge Crivelli painted in his picture, *The Annunciation*? It's not at all like Monet's bridge, is it? Look at the solid, powerful arch—you can tell that it would easily bear the people walking on it. Crivelli liked the architecture of the bridge. He explained every part of its construction—the supports, the arch, even the decorations.

See for yourself*

Do you begin to see that artists choose to paint in different ways? That's one of the reasons why looking at pictures is so exciting: painters show us all kinds of ways to look at the world we live in.
Find out how differently we all see things by playing a game with friends. Someone says, for instance, 'railway station'. Each player scribbles down the first words that come to mind. They might be as different as 'noisy', 'steamy', 'heavy cases', 'shiny engines'. Try the game with other words such as 'school' or 'football ground'.

Looking at nature

Here is a beautiful painting of a vase of flowers by the Dutch artist Jan van Huijsum (pronounced *How-zum).* Not many people could draw a picture as precisely as this! You can see every leaf and petal—even the spots on the eggs in the little nest. But the painting is not true to nature: you would never see all these flowers blooming at the same time.

Flowers in still life

It didn't matter to Huijsum that his picture is not true to a season. He wanted to say, 'Look at all the marvellous natural things we can enjoy!' Only he didn't use words to say this—he painted a picture of all the lovely flowers he could find. This painting is a *still life*—that is, a picture of deliberately-arranged things.

A bee's eye view

When you look at a piece of moss or a flower through a magnifying glass you discover a whole new world of intricate details and patterns. But what would you do if someone asked you to draw that flower? Would you put in everything you *know* is there, or would you only show what you can see with your naked eye?

Flowers in a Terracotta Vase
by Jan van Huijsum
painted 1736–7
size: 137 x 92cm

Movement in a pond

What was Monet trying to say about the flowers in his lily-pond? It's clear that he was painting a natural scene and not a still life, isn't it? Monet didn't show us any details in the lilies. We don't see all the petals and leaves the artist *knew* were there. Instead, we get an impression of dappled light falling on the flowers, and their lazy movement as the pond ripples in the breeze.
Monet was also interested in paint itself—its texture and variety of colours. How many different colours can you see in this patch of lilies?

Both Monet's and Huijsum's paintings are about nature. But each artist makes us see and feel something different.
All good paintings affect us in this way. They are a bit like music – we can sense what is going on without having to think it out.

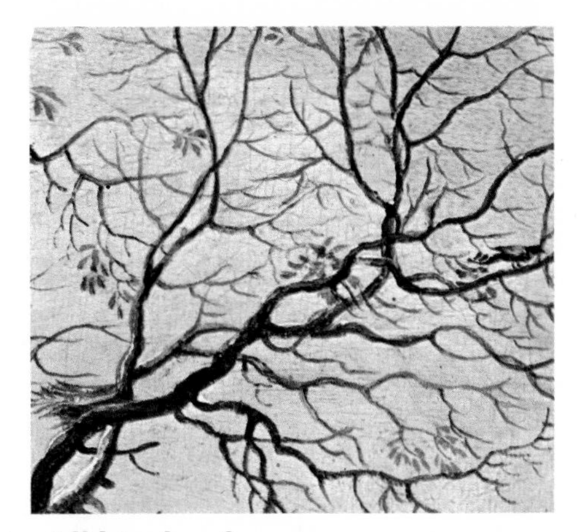

All kinds of trees

Sometimes a painter uses plants or trees to help set a scene or mood in a picture.
Look at the tree from Hendrick Avercamp's picture, *A Winter Scene with Skaters.* Its sharp outline tells us that the air is crisp and cold. The painting is really about skaters, but this bare tree helped the artist show the iciness of winter.
Below are some trees from Seurat's picture, *Bathers at Asnières.* See how the hazy sunlight shines on them? This tiny part of the picture adds to the feeling that it's a hot, still day on the river bank.

A little potted plant

You probably remember that the picture, *The Annunciation,* has people and buildings in it. But did you notice this potted plant on the balcony of Mary's house? The leaves are very precisely-drawn, and clear. And the pot is a lovely shape. Crivelli put this little still life detail into his painting to make Mary's house look real and lived-in.

Find the details*

There are other still life details in Crivelli's picture, including more potted plants, a piece of fruit and a vegetable. Look back to *The Annunciation* on page 11, and see if you can find them all.
Remember that you can look closely at a tiny part of the painting if you make two cardboard hooks as shown on pages 2-3. You could try using them to look at the still life details in Crivelli's picture.
(Did you also notice books, dishes, and a candle? These are still life details, too.)

All kinds of horses

Here is some action! Look how the hooves slip as the horse scrambles round the bare, dusty hill. This muscular animal and the equally tough cowboy work together, leaning into the hillside to keep their balance. See how Frederic Remington painted the mane and tail in rough brushstrokes? This gives the impression that the horse is really moving. The horse and rider look important—and lonely, too—because the background is painted with so little detail.

Today cowboys and cowgirls drive cattle across tame land. But when Remington painted this picture, the American Wild West still existed.

The Cowboy
by Frederic Remington
painted 1902
size: 102 x 70cm

Nobleman's steed

The Persian horse and its rider look very elegant indeed. There is something about the curve of the horse's neck that suggests it is a noble animal.

This horse is part of the story book illustration, *The Physicians' Duel*. But it doesn't seem 'alive'. The artist is more interested in the patterns and shape of the horse than in making you feel that it is real.

A Horse Frightened by Lightning
by Théodore Géricault
painted about 1820
size: 49 x 60cm

Look at the picture of a proud race-horse by Gericault. How beautiful he is! He looks fit and excited: his coat is so shiny and every nerve in his body is tense with anticipation. It's not just the way the artist has drawn the horse's body and legs that makes the animal look so alert. There's more to it than that.
A painter can exaggerate details to make a picture more exciting. This horse looks nervous—you can see the whites of his eyes. The painter also put in rumbling black clouds and a heavy sky for dramatic effect.
These details add excitement and tension. They make the horse seem more alive, more swift and energetic. In fact, although the horse is standing still, this picture seems to say, 'Look how fast and powerful the horse is!'

A horse in pain

This animal is all twisted and peculiar, not at all like horses look in real life. Yet you can definitely tell it is a horse—look at the outstretched neck and the bared teeth. You can hear the horse neighing very loudly in pain and fright.
Remember this horse from the picture, *Guernica*? The artist, Picasso, could have drawn it accurately if he wanted to. But he twisted the shape of the horse on purpose to make us feel the pain and ugliness of the scene.

Look at other animals*

Have you got a cat or a dog? Or does a friend have one that you could look at? If you wanted to tell people about it by painting its picture, what would you show? The alertness of its ears? Perhaps the joyful wag of its tail? Or the glossy coat and bright eyes of a very healthy animal?

How painters see people

Without using words, we tell each other lots of things. Your mother knows you aren't well, for instance, if you look 'a bit pale'. And what does blushing tell people?
The look or 'expression' on your face gives out an even clearer message. Add a gesture to a facial expression, and your message is clearest of all. What does a clenched fist say?
Artists have always known that the most expressive parts of the body are the face and hands.
Look below at the cartoon character. The artist, Patrick Hughes, made the cartoon figure look stupid by putting his eyes close together and by cutting off his head below the brain. And the gesture is unmistakable—he is sneering rudely at something.
This drawing is on the cover of a catalogue of modern paintings and the caption with it says, 'A child of six could do it!'
What do you think Patrick Hughes meant?

Portrait of a Man in Blue by Titian painted sometime between 1511–1576 size: 81 x 66cm

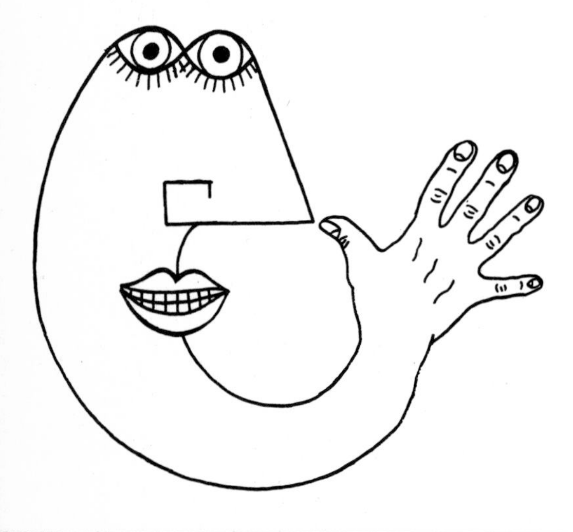

What is a portrait?

A painting which mainly shows a person's face is called a *portrait*. When you look at portraits made hundreds of years ago, you soon realise that people don't change much through the ages. Their dress is usually different, but their features or expressions often seem familiar.

Look at the man in blue shown here. His portrait was painted by an Italian artist named Titian (pronounced *Tish-un*) over 400 years ago. But you might see someone in the street today with a face—even a hairstyle—just like his.
The man has a mysterious, half-smile on his face. Is he pleased to have his portrait painted? Does he look vain as if he is saying, 'Well, I *am* a handsome fellow and now the world will know it'? Or does his expression tell you something else? Notice how his eyes seem to follow you wherever you sit.

One kind of perfection

Have another look at *The Annunciation*—the picture with the Virgin Mary in it—on page 11. Can you see how the painter made her face look delicate by painting fine lines for her eyes and mouth? She looks lovely. But her features are too perfect for you to feel that you would ever see a face like hers in the street! Crivelli painted her this way to show that she is holy and special.

Sitting in the sun

Compare the portrait of the man in blue with this boy's face from Seurat's painting, *Bathers at Asnières*. The man looks like a real person, doesn't he? The boy, however, doesn't seem to have a personality at all. His face has no expression—you can't even see his eyes or mouth. But you get the impression that the boy is feeling lazy and hot. See the reddish-blue tinge on his face? It looks very much like the colour skin goes in hot sunlight.

A face in torment

Here is one of those strange, frightened faces from the Picasso picture, *Guernica*. The woman's head is ugly. Her gaping mouth and outstretched neck show you the agony she feels because her child is dead. The face is disturbing partly because the eyes are so crooked and the mouth is much bigger than normal. Pablo Picasso exaggerated the woman's features on purpose, to show how horrible war is.

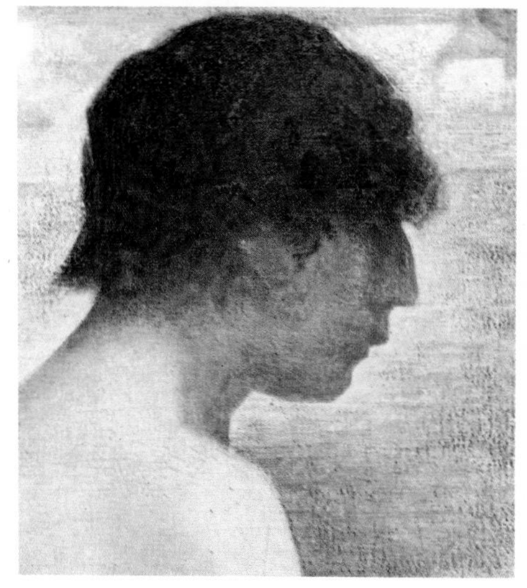

Add some modern clothes*

Collect pictures of historical people and see which ones look modern. An easy way to do this is to give the faces up-to-date clothes.
Cut a hole in a sheet of paper big enough to put the picture of the person's face underneath. Then draw a body wearing jeans and a T-shirt or a skirt. The result is sometimes very funny and surprising!

What clothes tell you

One of the things you notice when you look at pictures, is how artists paint in different ways. But you can also look at pictures as though they are 'photographs of the past'. You can discover how people lived in other centuries and other countries by studying the details of their clothes, the insides of their houses, the streets, and so on.

How do you dress?

At school you wear a uniform or everyday clothes. Maybe you wear the clothes you like best of all when you go out.
There are different clothes for different occasions. What you wear says something about you; *how* you wear your clothes tells even more.

Wealth and power

An artist knows that the way people dress can give us clues to who they are, how they live and what they are like.
Look at the portrait of Queen Elizabeth I of England. There is no mistaking the wealth and power of this grand lady. See the precious stones set into the band that runs down the front of her dress? Can you find a heart-shaped jewelled pendant on the band? And look at all the fine lace embroidered with gold streaming out behind the Queen's head.

This colourful painting shows us how a rich and royal person dressed in the 16th century. But history tells us that while Queen Elizabeth dressed in velvet and gold, the people of her kingdom wore plain wool tunics and rough cotton smocks.

Queen Elizabeth I
painter unknown
painted about 1585
size: 95 x 82cm

500 years ago

Here is the little girl peeping round the wall from the picture *The Annunciation*. What can you tell about her? She's clearly not poor and hungry—look at those plump cheeks! She is very neatly dressed, with a tight cap over her head and what look like pearls sewn round the edge of her pinafore dress. Perhaps she is the daughter of a rich trader or shopkeeper in town. And what is she dressed for? Maybe she is waiting for school to begin or for her parents to take her visiting.
These are questions which people who study history through pictures try to answer. Learning about the past is much more interesting when you know how people dressed.

Traders and peasants

You can see in *A Winter Scene with Skaters* that people dressed in different ways at that time. Two of the skaters are very richly dressed and obviously have lots of money. The other two people look very plain and simple and perhaps are farming folk from a village nearby.
Now look closely at the details. Do we use skates like these? And the hats—can you see that two are round and that one has feathers?

Luxury in Persia

Sometimes, of course, it is hard to tell if the painter is being truthful or just imagining fancy clothes. In the Persian picture, *The Physicians' Duel,* every courtier has gold decoration on his clothes. Do you think everyone could afford such costly embroidery, or was the artist just making his picture look pretty and decorative by putting patterns on all the colourful tunics?

Make a scrapbook*

Even the smallest detail in a painting can be interesting. You could spend hours in a gallery or a library just looking at such details as shoes, hats, and hairstyles.
Why not start a picture postcard scrapbook of different clothing? You could choose pictures showing the dress of a particular century or country. Or collect pictures of people in ruffs—the kind of stiff white collar the Queen is wearing. That would be unusual.

How keen are your eyes?

Now here's a chance to see what you have noticed in each of the pictures shown on pages 4–15 of this book. Here are the names of the six pictures again:

A Winter Scene with Skaters
The Physicians' Duel
Guernica
The Annunciation
Bathers at Asnières
Sinbad the Sailor

Can you guess which painting each of the details comes from? Before you turn any pages, here are a few clues.
Let's take the first detail which shows the little boat. One of the big pictures in this book is painted in blacks, whites and greys with strong, hard lines. That was *Guernica* by Picasso. But this boat is softly coloured, so it isn't from that.
There is a boat in the painting *Sinbad the Sailor* by Klee. Did you notice how it is made up of neat, flat, and distinctly-coloured shapes? The boat in the detail looks rounded, though, and has dark shadows painted on it, so it isn't from that one either!
What about the picture of the Virgin Mary and the Angel? It is very carefully and exactly drawn with lots of details in the buildings and clothes. So it can't be from that one!
Now you only have a few pictures left to think about. Which one shares the same colour and mood as the boat?

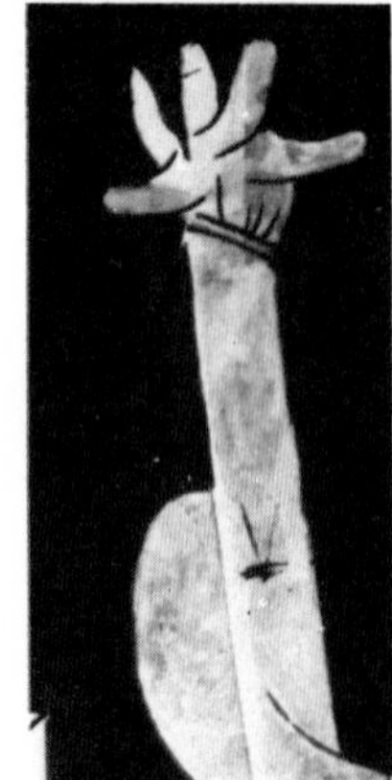

The painter's handwriting

All those differences you noticed are part of what is called a painter's *style*. Every artist paints pictures in a very special and individual way. It's just like handwriting. Perhaps you can recognise the writing of your best friend, your mother, or your teacher. Style is just another way of saying that an artist has a special kind of 'handwriting' when painting.

From cave wall to canvas

When you decide to paint a picture, you probably go into a shop and buy a box of water colours, or maybe even some tubes of oil paint. That's the easy part! But have you ever wondered what colours come from, or how paints are made?

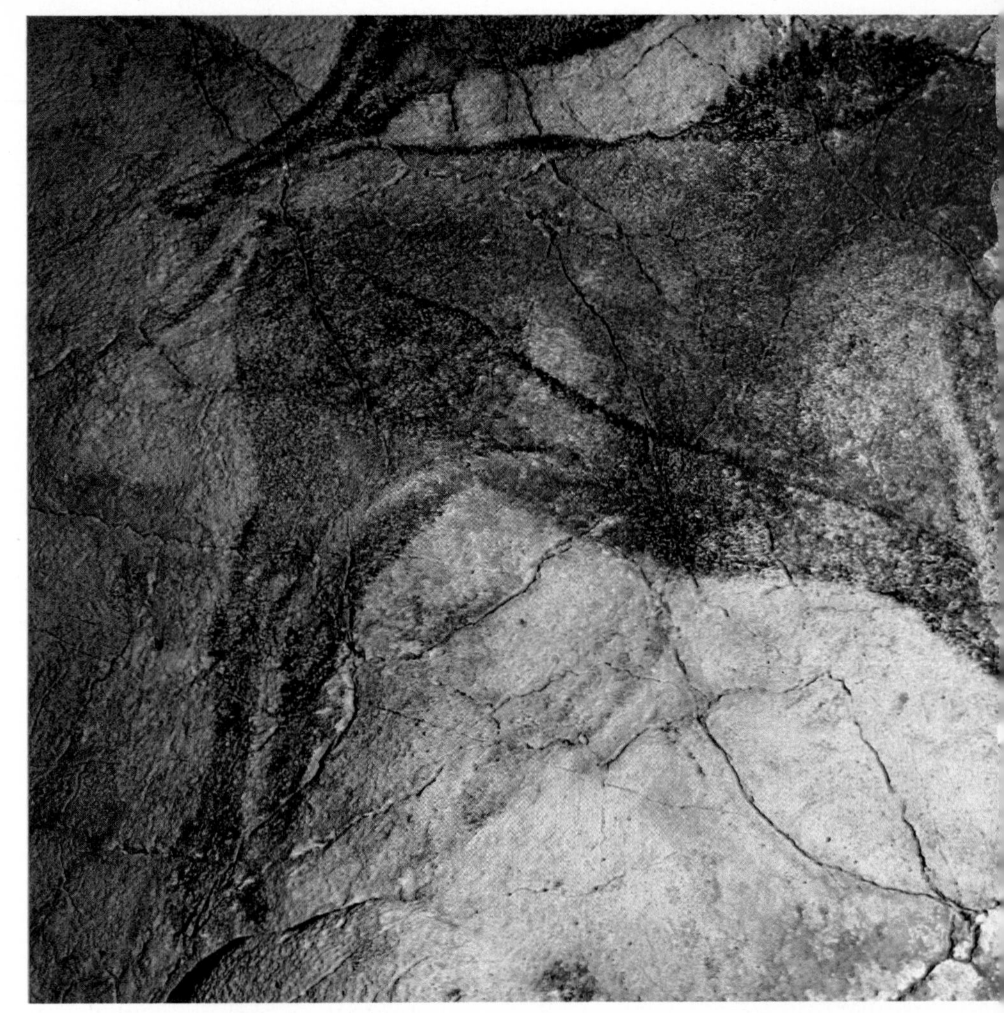

Altamira cave painting
painted about
20,000 years ago
size: about 77cm high

Nature's wealth of colour

Most colours are made from things in the natural world: earth, rocks, plants, precious stones and metals—even the dried bodies of insects.

To make colours, the raw material must first be ground to a powder called a *pigment*. Then the pigment is mixed with a *medium* to make it liquid and a *binder* to make it sticky. Water is a medium; oil (from seeds and flowers) is another. Gum (from trees and plants), glue and eggs are binders.

Remember the blue of the grinning doctor's robe in the Persian picture on page 7? It was probably made from a precious stone called lapis lazuli, crushed to a powder and mixed with gum to make a paint. A green pigment is ground from *terre verte* ('green earth') and a strong yellow comes from yellow ochre, a kind of clay. Raw Sienna—an earth found at Sienna in Italy—makes a clear delicate yellow. A lovely rose-coloured pigment comes from the powdered root of the rose madder plant. Scarlet is made from ground-up female cochineal beetles.

The world's first artists

Above is a picture of a prehistoric bison painted with colours made from natural things. It was put on a cave wall at Altamira in Spain, about 20,000 years ago. To make pictures like this, primitive artists first scratched an outline with a piece of flint, and then filled in the colour. They made brown, yellow and reddish pigments by grinding up iron ores with rocks. They mixed their pigments with plant juices or animal blood or fat to make them into paint. Black paint

was made from soot or charcoal, and white from chalk.
The artists put paint on with their fingers, or with brushes made from fur, feathers, or chewed-up twigs.
Can you imagine how much time and hard work it took to make a picture in this way?
Later on, artists began to paint on house walls, panels of wood, sheets of paper or very thin leather. Then, in the 15th century, artists began to paint on *canvas*. This is specially-treated cloth stretched tightly over a wooden frame.

The delicate touch

Look below at the Japanese picture of a kingfisher. See how transparent the paint looks? The paper almost seems to shine through those delicate blues and browns. That's because the artist has painted with water colour—a lovely soft, washy kind of paint. Water colours are made by mixing pigments with gum or water itself.
Yamanaka Shönen used only a few brushstrokes to describe the kingfisher. Yet it's very realistic and beautiful.

Kingfisher
by Yamanaka Shönen
painted sometime between 1806–1820
size: 27 x 19cm

Paints for every purpose

Today all kinds of paint come ready-mixed in tubes, and each type has different qualities. Water colour looks soft and transparent, when used. It's quite different from poster colour which gives a matt finish. Gouache (pronounced *goo-ash*) and tempera are opaque paints similar to poster colours. All these paints are used on paper.
Oil paint is thick and shiny, and is used to paint on canvas, wood, or special paper. Most pictures in this book were painted with oils. Because oil paint takes a long time to dry (between eight hours and two days!) many modern artists use quick-drying acrylic paints instead. These have the same glossy quality as oils.

Make your own paint*

You will need a stick of white or coloured chalk, two teaspoons of cooking oil, a chopping board and a metal spoon. (Ask before you use these things.) Break the chalk up, then grind it to a very fine powder with the back of the spoon. Add the oil, drop by drop, stirring the mixture until it is smooth.

A thousand and one colours

What is your favourite colour? Red, yellow, green or something else? Think about it for a moment, and then try to imagine how you would describe that colour in words. It doesn't help much to say, for instance, 'I like green'. One person might think of 'grass green' and another might think of 'bottle green'. There are so many different shades of colours and each one affects people in different ways.

Blue, blue or blue?

Think about the word 'blue'. List some different blues you've seen: sky blue, ink blue and perhaps cornflower blue.
Now look for blue things round your home, and try to think of the special word that tells you exactly how each one looks. How would you describe the blue of the man's sleeve on page 24 of this book? Smoky blue? Hyacinth blue? Sea blue?
If none of these fits, perhaps in the future you will think of that particular colour as 'Titian sleeve' blue!

Playing with colours*

You and your friends can play the word game with other colours: think of 'toast brown' instead of plain brown; or 'thundercloud grey' instead of ordinary grey. Each player scores one point for every new descriptive word.

Mixing basic colours

Red, yellow and blue are called *primary* colours. If you mix them in the combinations shown above you will make three *secondary* colours—orange, green and purple.
There are many kinds of red, yellow and blue. Try to find colours like the ones shown. The red is called magenta—it looks pink, but it is the best red to use for mixing.

Making shades of colour

If you mix different amounts of primary colours, you will get varying *shades* of secondaries. Get a magnifying glass and look at the secondary colours above. See how purple is made up of dots of blue and magenta red? Green has blue and yellow dots; orange has red and yellow ones. Browns are mixtures of all three primary colours.

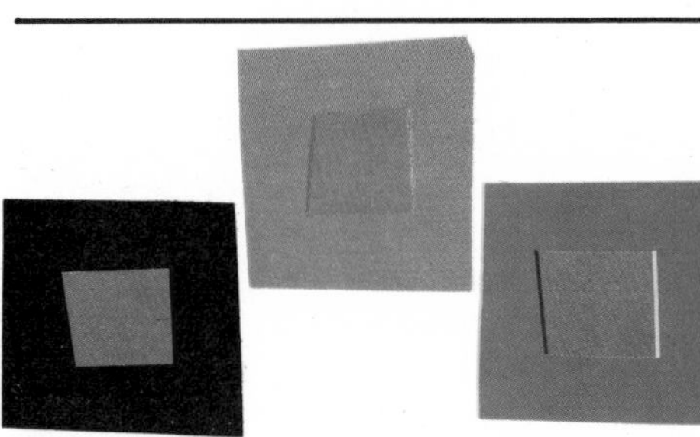

Experiment*

Put a scrap of red paper on white paper; then look at the red paper on brown. Which makes the red more vivid? Now try putting red on its opposite colour, green. See how different combinations affect your eyes? Colours look stronger when their opposites are present. So blue looks bluer when it is near orange; and yellow is stronger if it is near purple.

Match the colours*

Look carefully at the paints on these six palettes. Now think back to the six pictures shown on pages 4–15 of this book.

1. *A Winter Scene with Skaters*
2. *The Physicians' Duel*
3. *Guernica*
4. *The Annunciation*
5. *Bathers at Asnières*
6. *Sinbad the Sailor*

One palette matches the colours of one of these six pictures. Can you put the right letter with the right number? (Palette d has only black, white and grey on it, so you should be able to match that one! The answers are on page 44.)

a b c d

Opposite colours

The colours opposite each other in the centre of this wheel are called *opposite* colours: green and red; orange and blue; yellow and purple. (Sometimes they are called complementary colours.)
The outer circle shows just a few of the shades you can make by mixing different amounts of primary colours.

A dotty idea*

Remember how Seurat crowded little dots of paint together? And you have seen how dots make up secondary colours printed on this page. Try it yourself by making lots of magenta red and yellow dots; blue and yellow dots; blue and red dots. Stand four metres away and see what happens. You should be able to see orange green and purple.

The Snail
by Henri Matisse
painted 1953
size: 2·8 metres square

Here is a picture of coloured shapes on a white background. At first glance the arrangement of shapes looks very casual. But see how some of them curve round in a spiral, like the shell of a snail?
To make this picture Henri Matisse (pronounced *Ma-teece*), first painted his colours on separate sheets of paper, then he cut them out and stuck them down on a white background, just as a collage is made.
The colours are as carefully arranged as the shapes. Look how that big blue shape touches its opposite colour, orange. And how many red and green shapes can you see together?
If you still think *The Snail* looks casual, paint some sheets of paper; then try tossing the coloured shapes on to the floor. You'll see that Matisse didn't make his picture in this way!

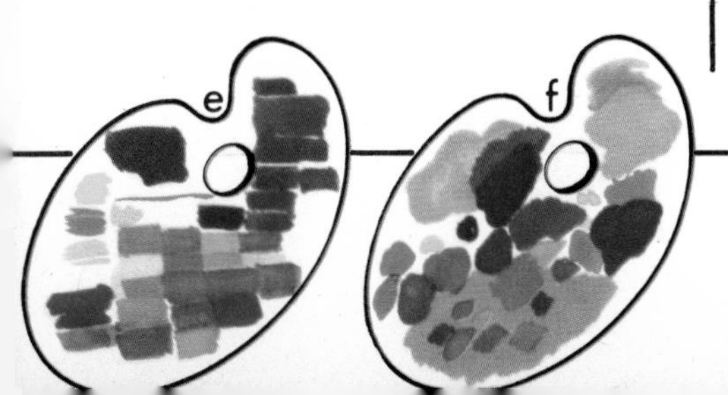

Perspective: magic... methods...

Do you feel you could walk into some pictures like Alice in 'Through the Looking Glass'? This is because the painters of these pictures use a visual method called perspective.
For hundreds of years, artists in Europe developed ways to create the impression that their pictures were not flat boards or canvases. They set out to make their pictures look like windows through which you could see into the distance.
Do you remember that when you describe a 'perspective' picture, the part that seems to be nearest the front is called the *foreground*? The most distant part is called the *background,* and the bit in between is the *middleground*? It's like looking inside a toy theatre with actors, scenery and a backdrop. The curtains in front of the theatre are like a picture frame.

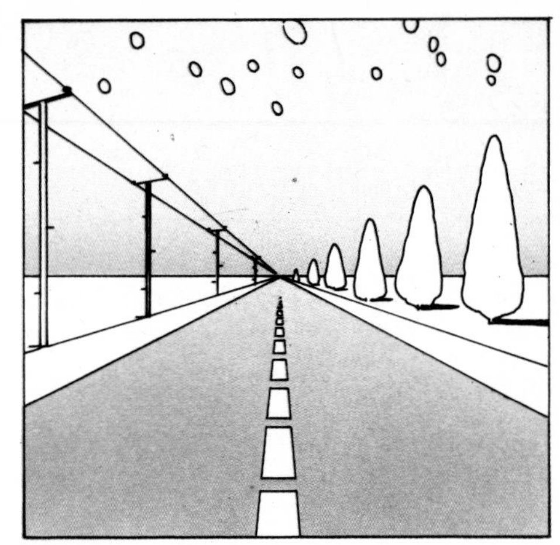

Lines

Painters create the effect of distance in five ways:
1. They use lines which would all meet at one point if you joined them up. (This is called linear perspective.)

Texture

4. They make textures like grass, fur or stony ground clear and recognizable in the foreground, but they make them muzzy in the distance (textural perspective).

or tricks?

Size

2. They draw the things in the foreground bigger than the same sort of things in the distance (perspective of scale).

Things in front

3. They draw people or things so that the ones in the foreground block out part of the things behind them (perspective of contour).

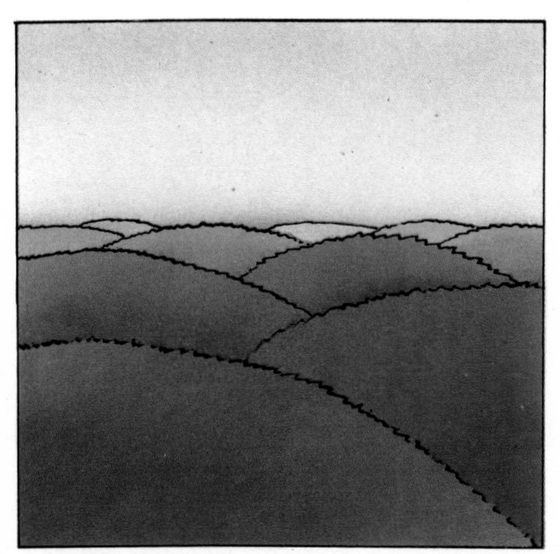

Pale distances

5. They use paler, bluer colours for things in the distance (aerial perspective).
However, some painters use only one or two of these methods and some do not use any at all.

Now add them together*

How many of the five perspective tricks are included in this drawing?
Have a look at other pictures in this book, and see if you can spot how many of the five ways each painter uses.

Hold up your thumb against some distant buildings. Which is bigger: your thumb or the buildings? You *know* that houses are bigger, so this drawing says they must be 'a long way away'.

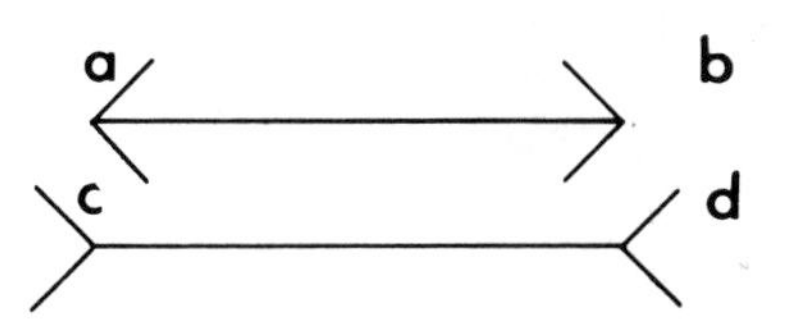

Now see how your own eyes can play tricks on you! Here are two lines **ab** and **cd**. Which looks longer?
Now take a ruler and measure each line.

Which cat is bigger and which is smaller? Use your ruler to check the answer. Can you see why your eyes tricked you? (A clue: it's something to do with the way the lines are drawn.)

Take a line for a walk

The artist, Paul Klee, once described drawing as taking a line for a walk. See the line 'walking' across the bottom of these pages? It begins as a slow, gentle curve; then it does a nervous little zig-zag. It becomes a thick wavy line, then a hard, sharp line, bending and turning in all directions. Suddenly it hops into tiny energetic dots, and eventually it wanders vaguely off the page. This line seems to have a personality of its own.

Start with a doodle

When you doodle with a pencil, you build lines up into patterns. Try it, and see! Is your doodle made up of geometric, coiled or spiralled patterns—or some other kind?
If you look carefully, you will begin to notice patterns in lots of different things.

See how the thin lines of this feather fan out from a strong central branch? Leaves have branch patterns, too. Look for spirals in pinecones, cobwebs and shells. Or make a print of the coils in your fingertip.

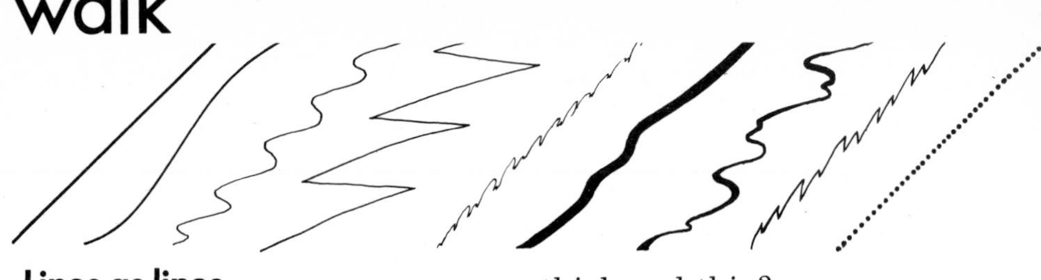

Lines as lines

Can you find here a straight line, a curved line, a wavy line, a jagged line, a dotted line? Which ones are thick and which are thin, and which line is both thick and thin?
Psychologists say they can tell a lot about a person's character and mood by studying the way he or she doodles, even with lines like these.

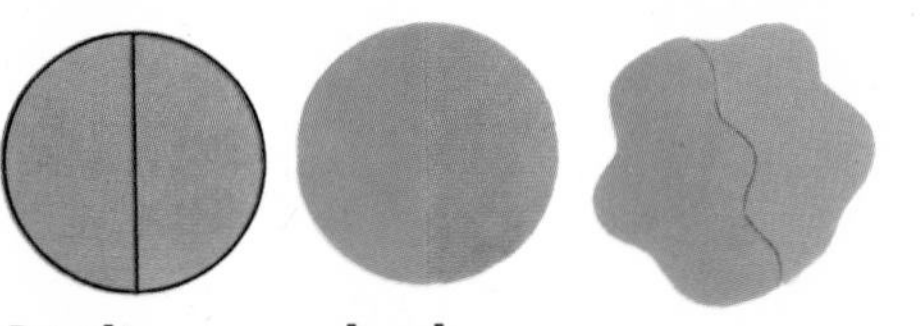

Lines as boundaries

You can create a line without actually drawing one, if you bring two colours together. Here is a boundary 'line' between orange and blue.

Outlines and edges

Drawn boundary lines look quite different, don't they? Colour can be used to create an edge too. Edges can be smooth, or rough, or blurred.

Something's fishy

Look at this detail from Klee's painting, *Sinbad the Sailor*. You can see the outlines of the fish, but the artist also used lines to make clever patterns. Do you think that the spiky lines suggest the scaly skin and boniness of fish?
Now look closely. Can you find Klee's signature on his painting? Klee deliberately signed his name in splintery lines to suit his picture.

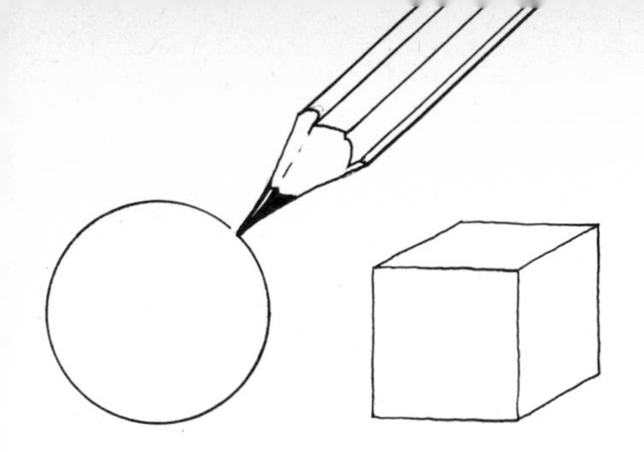

Lines as shapes

A line may describe a flat, two-dimensional *shape,* like this circle. Or it may describe a three-dimensional shape, like the cube.

All kinds of shapes*

See how many shapes you can draw in both two and three dimensions. Here are some suggestions: stars, clouds, cones, triangles, rectangles.

Lines as pictures

You can use words to describe something—say, a fish—or you can use lines. But when you make patterns, you are enjoying the lines themselves.

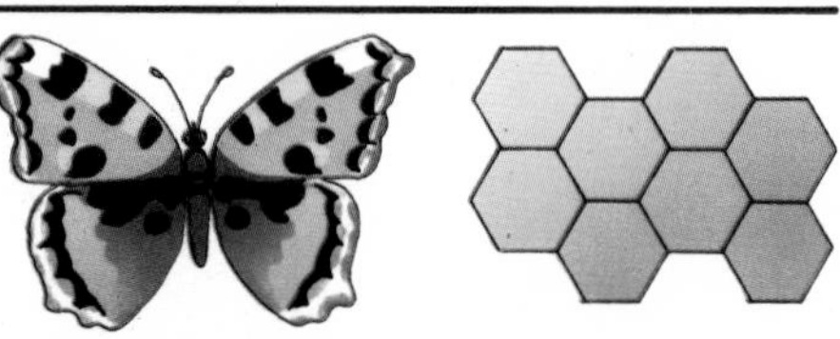

All kinds of patterns

Patterns can be random—like those in a butterfly's wing, or geometric—like this group of hexagons (six-sided shapes) that make up a honeycomb.

Painful lines

See how Picasso repeated short sharp lines in his picture, *Guernica?* The lines 'sound' like the rat-a-tat-tat of a machine gun, and they affect our nerves in the same way.

Beautiful geometry

In *The Physicians' Duel,* Aqa Mirak made beautiful patterns from lines. Can you pick out tiny circles, hexagons and six-sided stars around the throne and on the floor?

Find the lines*

Look back at the pictures in this book and see which artists have been interested in drawing lines. Both Klee's *Sinbad the Sailor* and Picasso's *Guernica* are almost entirely made up of lines.What about Crivelli's picture, *The Annunciation*? Look at this picture upside down to see the pattern of lines best.

Think of the big tree in Avercamp's picture, *A Winter Scene with Skaters*. The lines of the branches also make a very delicate pattern.

Remember Titian's portrait of *A Man in Blue*? There are no strong lines in it at all. But can you see where Titian created boundary lines between the blue sleeve and the dark cloak? Can you also find some boundary lines of colour in *Bathers at Asnières*?

There's one painting where you can hardly find any lines at all. The artist was more interested in the quality of light than in drawing lines. Can you find this picture? (There is a bridge in it, but even the lines of the bridge are vague.)

Shut your eyes and draw*

First, get a piece of paper and a pencil. Then shut your eyes and 'take a line for a walk' across the paper. It's just the same as doodling. Now open your eyes and see what your line looks like. How many words can you think of to describe the different lines you've drawn?

Light and shade

Using light and shadow is one of the most powerful ways to create a mood of drama or mystery in a painting.
The kind of pictures that spark your imagination or set you day-dreaming often have a marvellous quality of light. It might be gentle daylight, or a dramatic shaft of sunlight, or the mysterious glint of candlelight among shadows.

Gaining our attention

Sometimes artists use light to hold our attention. Look at Klee's painting, *Sinbad the Sailor,* on pages 14-15. See how the pale squares make a shaft of light that draws your eyes to the centre of the picture?

Light and shadow

You probably know that at 12 o'clock – when the sun is overhead – things cast hardly any shadow. But when light shines on an object from any other direction, a shadow is always cast.
Some painters use shadow to make people or things look solid or three-dimensional. Remember the shadows in the big blue sleeve on page 24? Or the shadows that show the muscles of the horse in the picture, *The Cowboy*?
Other artists are not interested in using light and shadow. Take another look at the rest of the pictures in this book to see which painters use light and shadow and which ones don't.

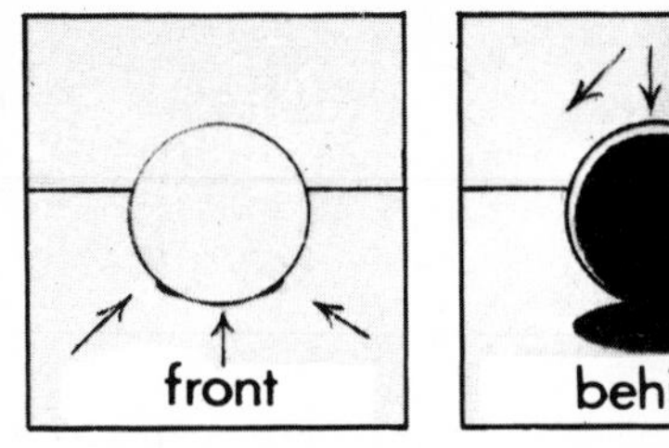

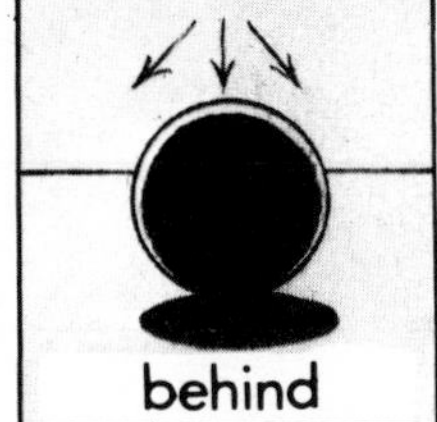

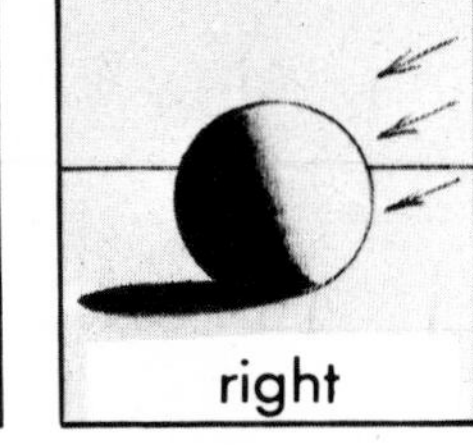

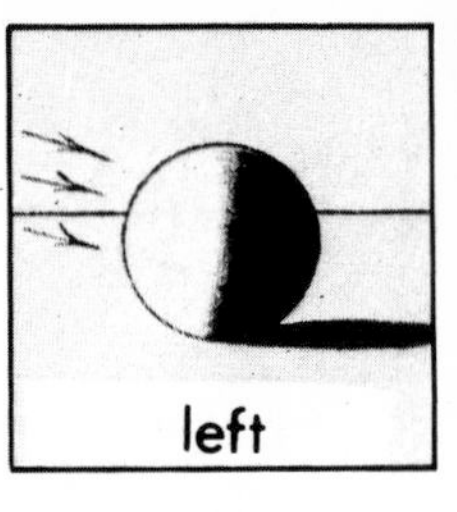

Making shadows

If you put a lamp or a torch in front of any object, you'll see: A shadow is cast behind it. Light from behind = shadow in front.

Light from one side = shadow on the opposite side. (Sometimes painters show the sun, or a candle or a lamp. But usually they 'suggest' the direction of the light.)

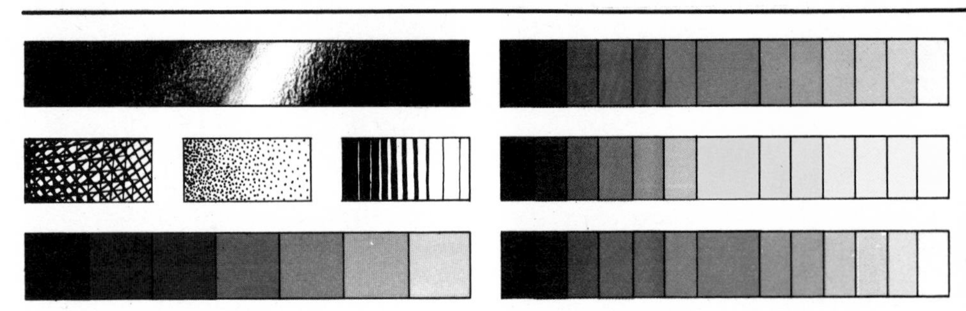

Shadowy greys*

Scribble heavily with a pencil, then more lightly, to get a few shades of grey. Or draw criss-cross lines in pencil, or lots of dots or stripes. Now see how many grey shades you can make by mixing different amounts of black and white paint together.

Shadowy colours*

When you add black or white to a colour, you change its *tone.* Try mixing up different amounts of white with blue. Then mix black with blue in varying amounts.
How many light tones and dark tones can you make by mixing?

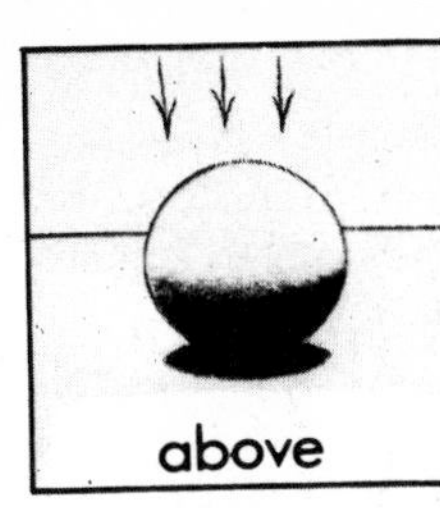

Light from directly above = almost invisible shadow below.
Light from below = shadow above.
Now experiment by lighting a person's face in several ways.

Follow the light*

Without the shadows, this tomato would look very flat. How can you tell that the light is shining from the right?
Now look at the three drawings below. Can you find the position of the light shining on each of these people?

The Man with the Golden Helmet
by Rembrandt van Rijn
painted about 1654
size: 67 x 50cm

Look at this man's magnificent gold helmet. It is bathed in glowing light, while the rest of the picture is sunk in dim reflections and deep shadows.

Rembrandt used candle-light to draw our eyes to details in the picture. See how the light picks up the tips of those feathers and the glitter of a gold shoulder-buckle? It also flickers across the man's face, just catching the expression in his eyes.
Can you work out where Rembrandt put his candle to paint this man's portrait?

Feeling without touching

Have you ever described something you've touched as 'hard', 'soft', or 'smooth'? These words tell people about the *texture* of that thing.
Everything has some kind of texture. Gravel feels rough and sand feels silky. Fried eggs are slippery and breakfast cereals are crunchy.
Sometimes you can sense how something feels simply by looking at it. You probably wouldn't ever touch an owl or a hedgehog, but you can *see* what those creatures would feel like. You would never actually touch a painting either, but you can often sense how things in the picture—or even the paint itself—would feel.
When you see a painting printed in a book, you can't always get a sense of texture. But if you go to a gallery, you could look out for all the pictures that make you want to reach out and touch them.

Swirling brushstrokes

Look at this picture of a starry night. See how the paint spirals, twists and rolls over the canvas? The real painting makes your fingers almost itch to touch it.

The artist, Vincent van Gogh (pronounced a bit like the Scottish 'loch'), loved both the texture of paint and the textures in nature. See how the surface of his canvas is lumpy? Look at the swirls of yellow paint—like great catherine wheels—racing across the sky. The cypress tree looks thick and snaky, too.

The Starry Night
by Vincent Van Gogh
painted 1889
size: 73 x 92cm

Here is Van Gogh's drawing of the same scene. Its surface is flat. But the vigorous lines tell you about the textures in the trees and fields.

As smooth as satin

Here is part of the portrait of the man in blue. You can sense, just by looking, how soft and shiny that big sleeve would be. The surface of Titian's picture, though, is very smooth. You can't 'feel' the texture of paint as you can when you see Van Gogh's picture of *The Starry Night*.
Notice the difference between Titian's soft curves and the distinct lines in the drawing by Van Gogh. Titian didn't use line to show texture. Instead, Titian makes you 'feel' the richness of the satin sleeve by showing you how it softly folds and crinkles as the man bends his arm. See the shadows in the curves of the glossy material? Titian used light and shadow to tell you about texture.

Make a collage*

Why not make a collage using natural textures? You could collect dead leaves, bark, ferns or grasses. Choose different colours and textures and arrange them on a sheet of white paper. Paste the things down with thick glue.
If you glue leaves or ferns on top of each other you can get a raised surface texture, just as Van Gogh did with paint.
You can also make textured collages with sandpaper and broken eggshells or scraps of velvet and satin.

Rub a texture on paper*

Place a sheet of paper on any textured surface and simply scribble over it with a soft pencil. You could rub over a brick, a coin, or a knotty piece of a wooden floor. You'll see lots of different textures and patterns. Or rub across the backs of leaves—then you can look at shapes as well as at textures in nature.

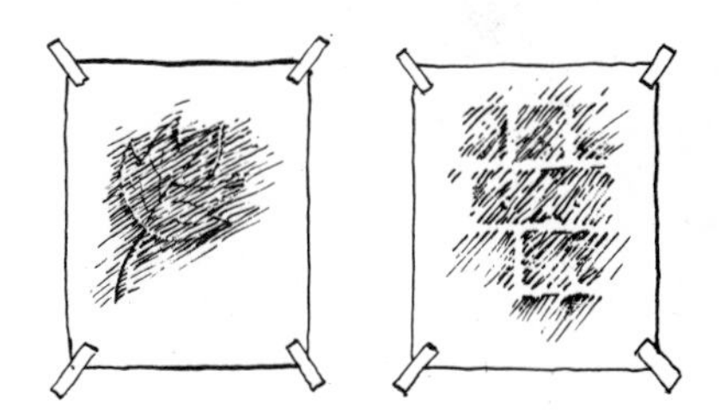

Putting it all together

If a hundred artists painted the same subject, you would see a hundred different pictures.
That's because every good artist thinks and feels differently about a subject. A painter may be inspired by an idea, but his real challenge is deciding the best way to put it across.
The first decision he makes is how to arrange everything in his painting. The proper word for the arrangement of things in a picture is *composition*.
To help him compose a picture an artist has colour, line, the five methods of perspective, light and texture. He might use one of these things, or a few of them, or even all of them! When he has made his decisions, he puts all the parts of his picture together on the canvas.

Balance

Here is one way of arranging things in a picture. Everything seems to be well-balanced in this drawing. You might think that such an arrangement is a bit obvious, but an artist can very easily focus your attention by putting things right in the middle of the picture.

Oops!

Another artist might want you to feel nervous and uneasy. He can do this by making the picture unbalanced. Of course, the canvas wouldn't *actually* tip up like this! But it gives you the idea of a painter who is deliberately crowding things on one side in a disturbing way.

Variations on a theme

The inspiration, the vision, the great idea—that's a painter's starting-point. The challenge is how to put it on canvas.
One artist may long to capture the wonders of nature. He might draw our attention to the roundness and beautiful markings of a snail, describing the tiny creature in exact and minute detail.

Another painter may be inspired by the thought of the dangerous life a snail leads, always afraid that a bird is going to pounce on it. (Luckily, snails probably aren't aware of their fate.) This artist might create a moody, dream-like atmosphere – a world of huge leaves and dark shadows where the snail must constantly watch out with alert, stalky eyes.

Harmony

Some pictures have a pleasing rhythm and harmony, just as music does. This drawing makes us feel comfortable and calm because of its harmonious composition. The figures are still grouped on one side of the picture, but now they are balanced by the tree.

Two portraits

An artist may decide to make someone look important by putting him right in the middle of the canvas. Now look at the drawing that shows the person slightly to the left. A painter might do this to make us feel puzzled or curious about someone's character.

Have you ever noticed how tiny and slow-moving a snail is? An artist may find that this appeals to his imagination and sense of humour. He might paint a picture that shows a funny little snail trying to get somewhere in a hurry.
Yet another painter could look at a snail and be fascinated by its spiral shell, starting small and getting larger.

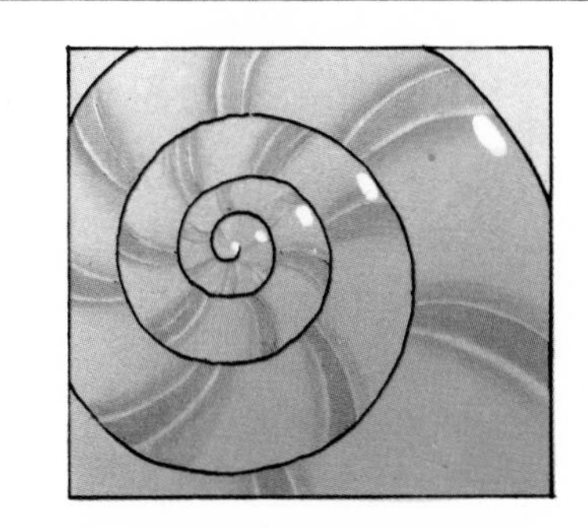

Can you imagine which parts of composition (perspective, line, colour, light, texture) each of these imaginary painters might use? Or where they might put the snail in their pictures?
Now look back to see how Matisse arranged his colourful shapes in a snail-like spiral. The white spaces in his picture are just as carefully arranged as the shapes themselves.

Compose things yourself*

Ask if you can have a piece of softboard or cork to hang in your room. Then think about arranging your pictures and other treasures on it. Arranging a wall panel is a bit like arranging things in a painting. When you look at your blank board, imagine you are an artist facing a blank canvas. Where to begin is quite a problem, even if you already have an idea of how your panel should look. First, place everything on the floor. Shuffle the things about to get a pleasing arrangement before you pin them into place. You'll find that there is a lot to consider: the sizes and shapes, colours, the spaces to leave in between, and where you want to put your favourite picture.

What next?

This book has been about noticing and enjoying pictures. But the original painting—the one actually created by the artist—is ten times more exciting than any reproduction. That's why going to an art gallery or museum is such an adventure.

Visiting art galleries

Find out where your nearest picture gallery is. You might already have been there on a school visit. But it's much more fun to go on your own or with a friend. That way, you have lots of time to stop and stare. And you can get really close to a painting that interests you, to see *exactly* how the artist has put his paint on the canvas. Some galleries also have special children's groups.

Keep looking!

Try going back on another day to look at a favourite painting again. You'll notice so much more the second time. Picasso once said that a picture only lives through the person who is looking at it. Part of the thrill of looking at pictures is finding something new each time.

Things to do

You can have fun in a gallery without making a noise, disturbing other people, or annoying the guard!

Chase a subject*

Hunt for pictures that show one of your favourite subjects—perhaps musical instruments, machines, cats or dogs, or mythical animals such as dragons and unicorns. Ask yourself which picture is the funniest, the strangest, the most exciting or appealing, and how each one is different.

Make some sketches*

If you're not too shy about other people looking, take a notebook and pencil and sketch the things that interest you. You could start a notebook of drawings of dresses or curious hats. If you are interested in buildings, you could do the same with window shapes, or chimneys, or roof-tops.

Use your view-finder*

Sometimes there's so much to look at in a gallery that it's hard to concentrate on one picture. And very often, big old-fashioned frames trick you into thinking that the pictures are dull and old-fashioned too.
Make a view-finder as shown on pages 2–3, and use it to blot out the frame and all other pictures. Hold the view-finder up and look through the hole. Then move backward or forward until all you can see is the picture.

Discover more

If you have enjoyed a particular picture in this book, why not read about the artist? Many of the great painters were like explorers because they discovered new ways to put across their ideas. Find out who discovered how perspective works, for instance, or who first used oil paints.
Take care of books. Make sure your hands are really clean, and always open a big book on a flat surface.

Starting a collection

Another idea is to make your own 'gallery' at home.
Start by cutting out pictures from magazines. Or buy cheap postcards and posters. Swap cards from galleries with friends or relatives in another town or country.
Collect pictures of one subject—say, ships or horses; or pictures by the same painter or from the same century.
Pin your collection to a wall panel like the one shown on page 43. Use dressmaking pins—these are better than drawing pins because they don't cover up so much of the picture.
After a while, you get used to looking at the same things, so keep changing your collection.
If you could have one of the paintings shown in this book for your collection, which would you choose? Ask yourself this question every few months and see if you come up with the same answer.

(Remember the palette quiz on page 32? Here are the answers: 1b; 2f; 3d; 4c; 5a; 6e.)